MERRY CHRISTMAS TO

....

FROM

....

WITH LOVE

FROM GOD WITH LOVE
published by Gold'n'Honey Books
a part of the Questar publishing family

© 1993 by Questar Publishers, Inc.

International Standard Number: 0-945564-78-3

Printed in Mexico

For information:
QUESTAR PUBLISHERS, INC.
POST OFFICE BOX 1720
SISTERS, OREGON 97759

93 94 95 96 97 98 99 00 01 — 10 9 8 7 6 5 4 3 2 1

From God With Love

HELPING CHILDREN
UNDERSTAND THE GOSPEL
THROUGH THE COLORS
OF CHRISTMAS

BY MACK THOMAS
ILLUSTRATED BY STEPHANIE BRITT

*In the Bible, you can find the Christmas story
in Luke 2:1-20 and in Matthew 1:18–2:13*

Gold 'n' Honey
BOOKS

CHAPTER 1

IF WE HAD BEEN THERE...

If we had been there on that
   first and greatest Christmas—

and if we knew then
   what we know now—

            we would say…

"That's right, angels!
Sing out for joy!
Make your mighty music
for the Baby born tonight!"

And we would say…

"That's right, shepherds!
   Hurry on to Bethlehem!
   Find that Baby
      whom the angels sing about—
        Jesus, the Son of God!"

               And we would say…

Yes, those would be
our very own words…
if *we* had been there.

SAY!
Let's pretend we *were* there!
Let's all go back
and be Christmas people—
on that first and greatest Christmas
long ago.

And we won't forget
what we know now!

CHAPTER 2

WHAT WE KNOW NOW...

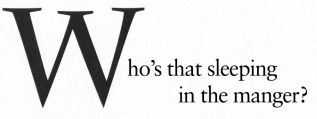ho's that sleeping
in the manger?

Yes…the Baby Jesus,
sweet and good.
And see the manger—
rugged and rough,
and made of wood.

Oh yes, don't forget the wood…
Because we know this
about the Baby in the manger:

When Jesus grows up—
    when He's a Man,
        brave and strong—
people will put Him on a cross
    that's rugged and rough,
        and made of wood.

They'll nail Him to that wood—
    Jesus our Savior,
        brave and good.
Jesus will die, and be buried in a tomb.

But *tonight* is the night
when Jesus is born…
And out on the hillside
the sheep are asleep
and maybe some shepherds,
too. Then suddenly—

So much light!
The sky is filled with heavenly light—
        blazing, amazing light!

An angel is here to tell us good news:
        The Savior is born tonight!

Oh yes, don't forget the light...
Because we know this:
        When Jesus grows up—
                when He's a Man,
                        brave and strong—
        there'll be *another* blaze of light...

But now is the time
when Jesus is born...
See the wise men!
They travel so far.
They follow a star
to Bethlehem.

They look for the Baby
who's born a King.

Where is the King?
They want to see Him.
They want to know Him.
They want to worship Him.

They found Him!
God helped the wise men find Jesus—
    the Baby who's born a King.

The wise men looked for Jesus
    and that's why they are wise.

Oh yes, don't forget to look for Jesus!
    Because we know this:

Always and forever,
everyone who is wise
will look for King Jesus...
to find Him,
and worship Him.

King Jesus was born
at Christmas.
He came down
from God's Heaven
for everyone,
as a gift to you and me…

a gift from God,
with love.

CHAPTER 3

TO HELP US REMEMBER...

So now, when we see the
Christmas colors—

gold,
white,
red,
and *green*—

we'll remember what they mean…

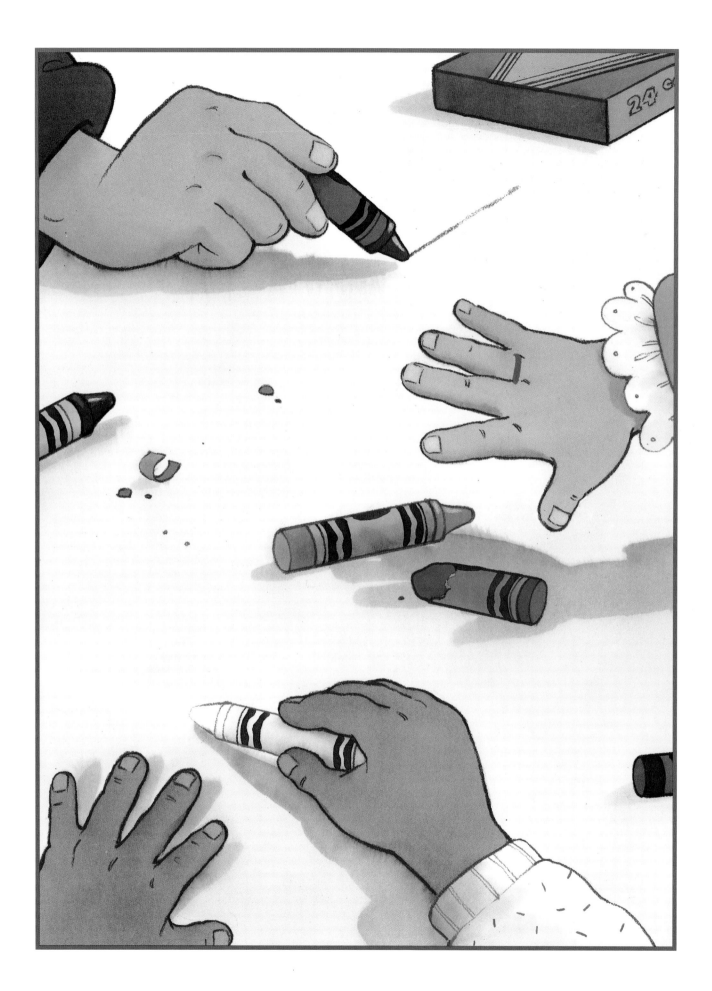

Look all around…
Where do you see the color *gold?*

Christmas gold is like Heaven.
Heaven is God's home,
    where the streets are glassy gold.
Heaven is always bright
    with golden light.

In Heaven no one cries,
    and no one is sick,
        and no one gets hurt.

    And Heaven is where God
        wants *us* to live someday.

But there can be nothing bad
in Heaven's light—
no bad things,
no bad words,
no bad thoughts.

In God's bright Heaven
there can be *nothing* wrong…
and *no darkness*
like the black winter night.

But sometimes you and I
do bad things and say bad words,
and think bad thoughts.
So how can we ever go
to God's bright Heaven?

Christmas *red* shows the way!
Red is the color of Jesus's blood
    when He died for you and me—
        when He died on the cross of wood.

When Jesus was nailed on the cross,
God put all this on Jesus:
    all the bad things we do,
        all the bad words we say,
            all the bad thoughts we think…
everything bad!

That's why Jesus died
    and was buried in a tomb.

Everywhere,
everywhere,
Christmas red!
But we know that Jesus
rose up from the dead!
And now He lives
in Heaven's gold.
He'll never be dead again.

And look!
	Where do you see the color *white?*

Jesus makes us clean inside,
	as clean as Christmas white,
		as clean and bright as snow.

With a Christmas prayer to Jesus,
	we can be clean like snow.
Then someday we can go and live
	with God
		in Heaven's gold.

So here's
a Christmas prayer
for you and me:

Lord Jesus,
I've done bad things,
and said bad words,
and had bad thoughts.
But this I know:
You died for ME.
Forgive me for being bad.
Come live inside my heart,
and be with me forever.

And look!
    Where do you see the color *green?*
There it is!
    In Christmas trees and holly—
        things that grow!

And *we* can grow in a special way
    when Jesus lives inside us.

As we get to know Jesus in the Bible,
    we can grow wise and
            good and strong.

Christmas *green*, Christmas *red*,
Christmas *white* and *gold*—

in all these colors a story is told…

a story from God, with love.

*For God so loved the world
that He gave His one and only Son,
that whoever believes in Him should not perish
but have eternal life.*

JOHN 3:16